Victim
Survivor
Thriver

Healing from Sexual Assault

Katrina L. Owensby

ISBN: 9798359487559

DEDICATION

To those who've made the creation of this book possible-
To all my angels-
To all my guides-
To all my supporters-
To my true family-
To the victims-
To the survivors-
To the thrivers-
This one's for you.

CONTENTS

INTRODUCTION

Dear reader,

Hello, my name is Katrina, but I have preferred to be called Kat since the incident, and I am a thriver of sexual assault. When I began writing this book, it was for a final assignment in my last writing course at college. My professor told our class that we needed to write a nearly completed non-fiction book on the topic of our choice. Trust me, I tried thinking of any other topic than being sexually assaulted and healing from it when I was given this assignment, but my heart wouldn't let me write about anything else. I needed to write about something meaningful in order to get through the semester, and this was the topic that repeatedly came to my mind. So, here I am, the summer after taking this class, having graduated, and I still can't get this book out of my head.

I wrote this book from the point of view of someone who has experienced sexual assault speaking mainly to those that have shared similar experiences. Seeing as roughly one in three women are sexually assaulted at least once in their lifetime, this is a book I feel very passionate about sharing, regardless of how difficult it was to write. To be completely transparent, some of the content shared in this book is triggering, especially within the first two sections, so I encourage you, as the reader, to approach this book as you would the amusement park. Think of the beginning and end of this book as the entrance and exit of the park and each poem as a ride. If you'd like to start from the entrance and ride all the rides in the order that they come, then do so. If you'd like to skip around the park and ride various rides based on what you're drawn to, then do so. If you're ever queasy during a certain ride or feel as though you aren't ready to go on a ride, then you have the power and control to simply stop, take a break, and go back to it later or simply continue on to a different ride.

This book is centered around the "Victim, Survivor, Thriver" model that my therapist introduced me to back in 2019. To give a short explanation, once a person experiences trauma, they are immediately set into the category of "victim". In this stage, the person may feel confused, broken, hopeless, and/or in denial.

Then, as the person heals, they will advance into the category of "survivor". As a survivor, the person may feel stuck with their emotional pain, learn to use coping mechanisms, be able to label what happened to them, and/or have hope in their healing. Through consistent hard work and healing, a person will then move into the category of "thriver". In this stage, a person may live in the present, have insights into the trauma they faced, not feel broken, and/or help others through their healing processes. Healing is not linear, so not all the poetry written in the "Victim" and "Survivor" sections are necessarily written chronologically.

I recognize that everyone's experience with sexual assault, be it personally or not, is different. This is just my story and my experience with healing. I wrote this book as a way for others that have experienced similar traumas to have an idea of what healing may look like for them, introduce various coping mechanisms they may like to use, or even for those that have never been sexually assaulted to better understand what this trauma and healing process is like from a thriver's point of view. Throughout my healing process, I wrote poetry to cope with my experiences, including the trial that occurred years after I was assaulted. This is just a part of my story, as all our traumas are a part of us. So, dear reader, I invite you into this part of my life, including the trauma and the healing, and the good and the bad.

Yours truly,

Kat

Section One- Trauma

Part 1- The Incident

The Fragmented Nightmare

That night, the Friday before classes started my senior year, it was my first time at a bar.
(I was eighteen at the time and the bar allowed people 18 years and older.) I was hesitant to go. My roommate convinced me everything would be fine, and I believed her. Before we did much that night, my roommate, her friend, and I all went to her car to drink. It was one of my first experiences drinking and I didn't have much knowledge about alcohol. I drank way too much and got way too drunk.

I wasn't trying to get drunk.

I met him on the dance floor of the bar. At this point, the room was spinning, and my balance was leaving me quickly. My roommate handed me my phone and told me to meet her and her friend outside the bar at a certain time.

I was too drunk to read the time on my phone.

He offered to walk me home. My brain was so jumbled that I couldn't grasp the danger that was in that question when I allowed him to. I could barely stand up. There's footage of me nearly falling over multiple times on the walk to my dorm. There's footage of me stumbling into the side of the elevator door in my old residence hall.

I was too drunk to walk.

I don't remember how I got there, but the next thing I can know, I was on the futon in my dorm room, a dorm room I had just barely moved into. He was on top of me and had pulled my dress above my hips and pushed my underwear to the side. I tried to get up because I knew that something was wrong. He took his right hand and pushed my left shoulder down. I didn't really know what was happening to me until the next morning, but I knew it was wrong and I knew I couldn't fight it.

I was too drunk to fight it.

The next thing I remember was waking up to my roommate and her friend walking into the dorm. I was in the same position on the futon. I pulled my dress below my hips. My roommate was upset that I didn't meet them outside the bar like she had planned. I was so disoriented. I don't know how I made it up to my loft to go to sleep that night. I just know that I woke up to a nightmare the next day.

Even after it happened, I was too drunk to realize what he did.

This is all I can remember of the assault. I spent so many nights shifting between wanting to forget and wanting to remember everything so that maybe, just maybe, I could move on. It's not that simple though. That was my first sexual experience. An experience I wanted to save until I got married. An experience that was taken away from me by a complete stranger.

Is it even considered sex if I was too drunk to consent?

A Goodbye to Innocence

I tell you I cannot stay.
I must go away.
I hope to visit you again,
someday,
along a sanded beach.
Moment by moment
I shall try
to grasp you in my arms again,
but never shall I reach
the beautiful depths of your soul.
My beloved,
I'm sorry I didn't cherish
each moment,
each breath
I had with you.
My lost beloved,
my dearest friend,
hopefully we'll soon meet again
in paradise.

When My Eyes Opened

I woke up the next day, my body was hot from the
summer sun coming in through the dorm window,
and I groggily tried to piece together
what happened the previous night.
It wasn't until I looked at the purity ring on my
finger that I remembered what he had done to me.

It is difficult for me to even begin to convey the emotion
that I felt at that moment. I suppose it was a mixture of
panic, fear, helplessness, and disbelief. I had never felt
something so strongly wrong within myself. I knew the
pain of losing loved ones, but never the pain of
losing such a precious part of myself.

I remember crying quietly so that I wouldn't wake my
roommate next to me. I remember going to my best friend's
dorm in the same building and telling her I had been
raped. I remember her hugging me as we both cried. She
called her mom and asked what we should do.

No one ever tells you what to do when you get raped.
No one tells you what it does to you.
No one ever prepares you for what happens
after.

They barely told me how to avoid such a situation.
They told me not to wear provocative clothing,
maybe that will save me.
They told me not to walk alone at night,
maybe that will save me.
They told me not to get into
cars with strange men,
maybe that will save
me.

That morning, I was beyond saving.
What could they tell me now?

My friend's mom told me to tell my RA,
call my parents and go to the hospital.
How was I expected to share such a
traumatizing experience with others when
I hadn't yet fully processed what had
been done to me? How was I supposed to
tell my RA, a girl I had met days before?
Or tell my parents?
Oh God, how was I
supposed to tell them?
Broken-
That girl was so broken.

The Hospital

I can't hold back the tears when I
call my mom and dad.
My mom answers,
I tell her what happened to me.
She cries.
She tells me they're going to
drive to see me
as soon as they can.
She has to call my dad,
who was golfing at the time,
and tell him to come home
because something happened to me.
They drive 1 ½ hours to take me to the
hospital.

The trauma nurse escorts me
to a room away from my parents.
She asks me if I want an advocate,
someone to walk me through
the process and support me.
Numbingly, I say yes.
My voice doesn't sound like
my own anymore.
Once the advocate arrives,
she explains what would occur
during my time in the hospital.
I'm paralyzed in fear.
I let a tear escape.
I wipe it away before they notice.

In the hospital, they ask me
so many graphic questions.
I was questioned
-once from the doctor
-once from my parents
-once from the detective
-once from the city police
-once from the campus police.
I laid on my back
on top of a cold

hospital exam table.
I wonder how they
expect me to answer
all these questions
while I'm still in shock.

They examine me.
All of me.
They take pictures of
my body for evidence.
The trauma nurse swabs me
for his DNA.
She puts the swab, along with
documents and photographs
describing and showing my injuries,
into a rape kit in case I decide
to press charges when they find him.
When they find a man I don't even know.
The nurse tells me the kit
will be sent three hours away
and good for one year,
as though she's discussing the
warranty on a household appliance.

The trauma nurse says we are
almost done and that I'm doing
an amazing job at pushing through.
The advocate tells me that
my parents are crying in the waiting room.
She says they just want me to be okay.
I'm sad that I can't reassure them I am.
I am anything but okay.
The advocate reassures me
that I am doing so well at staying strong,
but I feel so hollow.

Once everyone is done examining
and questioning me, and the advocate
has finished her explanation of
what to expect next and what resources
are available to me (all of which are detailed in
a large folder),

we drive back to the dorm, where it happened,
in silence.

When I get back to that room,
I realize that I haven't eaten yet.
I don't think I could even if I tried.
My parents leave at my request.
I'm left alone,
in fear,
in tears.
I don't know what time it is,
but I go to bed.
I hope that if I fall asleep,
when I wake up,
it'll all just be a bad dream.
However, when I try sleeping,
I just stay awake, seeing him
everywhere I look.
I cry silently, hoping my roommate
doesn't hear my pain.
Did I sleep that night?

Day Two

I get up for the day.
I make calls to my closest friends.
"How could this happen?"
I avoid food all day.

My parents call.
"Are you okay?"
"Yeah, sure."
They want to pull me out of school
two days before the first semester begins.
I refuse.
My purity ring burns my finger.
My fault? No.
My choice? No.
Please God, don't hate me.
Maybe I could've…?
Stop!
Unproductive thoughts.

My advocate calls.
I have an appointment
for an interview
with a detective.
Pressing charges is
what you're supposed to
do when this sort of thing
happens, right?
She asks how I am holding up.
"Fine."

I'm bleeding.
He hurt me.
It is painful to use the bathroom.
It is painful to exist.
I remember that I'm free to shower
now that the rape kit is done.

The campus police come.
They take my clothes from yesterday.
They take the futon and blanket.

They tell me that they have to
interview my roommate.

I guess I was forced to
become one in three women
before I even started college.
I barely slept that night.
I never stopped
feeling his hands on me, and
seeing his haunting shadow.

But I also saw a butterfly that day…

Section Two- Victim

Part 1- Disrupted Identity

After Trauma

They say that after a person
experiences trauma
their mind changes
they are a new person
I don't get a choice of who
I have become
and I hate it
I hate this person
She is not me
She is reckless
and irresponsible
and not
at all
me
When can I have myself back

Broken Tenant

I'm living
in an old version
of myself-
I've outgrown
my dwelling place-
alienated
in a place
that should be
my home-

mourning me

i should wear black
everyday
a symbol
of the death
of the happy girl
i once was
where is joy
where is she
where

i'm so far gone
i can't even cry
to cleanse
my hurting soul

Medusa Dreams

A few weeks after I was assaulted,
I began to have these strange dreams.
In these dreams, I was chased by
a village of people on a boat
that was stranded on land.
When I escaped the boat
and looked at my reflection in a window,
I wasn't myself anymore,
I had turned into Medusa.

These dreams felt so vividly real
that I decided to research Medusa's story.
Mythology states that Medusa was
assaulted by Poseidon in Athena's Temple.
Upon finding this out, Athena turned
Medusa into the snake-like creature
that she's remembered as today.
Was she given the power to turn
men into stone to protect herself
or was she cursed to never get close
to another person for the rest of her life?

I came to find that the boat on land
symbolized me facing
a time in my journey where I
experienced setbacks.
I didn't just look like Medusa,
I had become Medusa.
I was forcibly embarking on
a treacherous journey and I
feared I had lost myself forever.
Would I tap into my power
or would this moment be forever
considered a curse for me?

Medusa: The Woman

I once was beautiful,
full of light.
My sole gaze could
enrapture an entire city;
but life is merciless,
so my innocence didn't save me.

See me? I'm not a monster.

My beauty turned to repulsiveness,
and my hair,
the thing she envied the most,
into venomous snakes.
Men, captivated by my charm,
are now fossilized by one glimpse
because of one man's uncontrolled lust.
Loneliness and torment were thrust upon me.

See me, I'm not a monster.

My life is an epic tragedy.
Maybe I should mangle my snakes,
and gauge out my offensive eyes.
Torture me for being senselessly punished;
or perhaps I should just wither away…
maybe then you will

see me: I'm not a monster.

Unreachable and Intangible

There are colors
that I cannot touch.
There are sounds
that I cannot feel.
        Why can't I feel?
I used to be so happy-
I used to be…
Even my handwriting isn't
mine anymore
        -forevermore?
I feel sick.
        Am I sick?
        Am I what I feel?

Shadow Hands

There are shadows
        on my hands
Always shadows
        never just light
Light is obscured by
        those shadows
Light is dimmed
        and faint
Light will soon be gone
Light will soon give up
        on my hands too

Covered by shadows
        are my hands
Those hands they say
        are mine
How are they mine
        when I can't feel them
My hands are so numb
        and close to gone
My hands are just like
        everyone
        everything
                because they're gone
                        always gone

But at least there is still light somewhere…

To the Girl Inside

To the girl inside,
Wake up already
I've been calling you
For what feels like years now
From,
Your last piece of hope

To the girl inside,
Why won't you come out
I'm suffering here
Screaming for you
From,
Your last piece of hope

To the girl inside,
I'm crying for you to come
Out into the open
Why won't you listen
From,
Your last piece of hope

To the girl inside,
Everyone wishes you were here
So please
Awaken for me
From,
Your last piece of hope

Part 2- Unsteady Socializing

Social Life SOS

I was warned before I went to college
that making friends would be difficult.
For the first time in my life,
I had complete control over
who I socialized with.
However, that control left me
every time I was faced with a trigger.
My body forced me to leave
classes,
movies,
coffee shops,
libraries,
and everywhere else
I was reminded of him
and what he did to me
How was I supposed
to make friends
when I couldn't even
make myself heal?

Common Triggers for a Victim

1. That consent training that's required at the beginning of the school year
2. Nighttime
3. Loud noises
4. People standing behind me
5. Shadows
6. People touching my left shoulder
7. Anyone touching me in general
8. Dorm rooms
9. The topic of sexual assault
10. Catcalling
11. Hugs
12. Late summer nights
13. The mention of his hometown
14. Seeing someone that even remotely looks like him
15. Hospitals
16. Visits to the OB/GYN
17. Darkness
18. Laying on my back
19. Hearing his name
20. Being alone

Fear of Insanity

They ask me,
"What's wrong?"
and I'm afraid to say
I feel like I'm going
insane.
It's getting worse-
the voices-
the shadows-
The voices are louder
and
the shadows have
manifested into
people-
unrecognizable and yet
they seem so real.
So yes, when they ask me,
"What's wrong?"
I simply say,
"Nothing."

"The Kitchen is a Woman's Place" Carries a New Meaning for Me

My kitchen holds the
depression
my body is too
ashamed to show.
I wonder how
my dishes have piled up
in a monstrous heap
when I can't even
force myself to eat.
My trashcan spills over
from the mess I hide so well.
No visitors come inside to wonder
what went wrong and when.
There's a dangerous reassurance
when the only visitors
who dare to explore deeper
are those that are only concerned about
physical figure.
My heart is imprisoned in
the weight and the dark pressure on my chest
is the sole reminder I'm alive.
Yet, I feel like I (whoever I may be)
am floating somewhere above
my form
displaced
distressed
damn near
dead

Catcalling Kids

I got really mad at these kids in the mall
because I heard them catcalling young girls.
I had to say something before
catcalling became something…
more.
That scares me.

Catching Up

Catching up with old friends
is difficult
when you've been through so much
since the last time you've seen them.
Do I smile and fake happiness?
Do I cry and show my pain?
Do I laugh and lie to my heart?
Do I remain truthful and ruin the mood?
I ask myself these questions
all because of you.
I hope you know that.

Ironic Intimacy

They asked me what it was like
when I did ~it~ after that ~thing~
happened to me.
I told them it was like I wasn't even
in my body, not floating above or around
like some people say, but I felt like my
body was a shell.
No, not a shell, maybe like cling wrap.
Yeah, like cling wrap.
I was inflated with air
and my edges were seared together to
make a bubble. A bubble of cling wrap.
Neither floating nor sinking. Stuck in time.
Every time they were on top of me,
they'd gouge a hole in the plastic.
So, I'd twist the plastic smaller to fain
an image, but each time the cling wrap bubble
got smaller and smaller, the shell of me
got smaller and smaller 'til I was nothing.
I was nothing
I was nothing
I was nothing

Dorm Tears

Crying in your dorm is
the worst.
You try to muffle the sobs
so no one knows you're in pain.
You wish you could call someone,
anyone,
but you're afraid that they'll be scared
of how messed up you are.
You lock the door
so that maybe you'll have enough time
to wipe your tears
before your roommate comes in
and you say,
"I'm fine."

Part 3- Mental Oubliette

Anger Fuels my Mental War

my mind is at war
and it's as though
every one of
my thoughts
my feelings
my memories
my dreams
have become soldiers
shooting
at each other

equilibrium is
lost
it's simply
good
versus
bad

I'm afraid to
discover what
soldiers I've lost
but I'll only realize
once the war
has ended
and it's all too late

there will be no peace treaty
and surrender is impossible

Despite my efforts
to prevent it anger
has become the shield
I use
to ensure that
I'm left alone

No one can hurt me
if I scare them away first
right?

French Final

Here I am,
sitting in my French final.
I should be worried about
failing
or
passing.
Instead,
all I can think about
is what you did to me.
When will it ever get easier
to live my life
and push away
these awful memories?
When will I ever
live again?

Moving Back

I'm moving back home
forcibly
because of you.
How can you still be controlling
my life
all these months later?
More tears come
because of you.
How can I rid myself
of your control?

But I guess moving back is still moving nonetheless and that's better than stagnation…

Unquantifiable Pain?

How do you quantify pain?
Not physical pain that is
temporary,
but a pain that is inescapable-
a pain that cannot be summed up
in words.

How do I express the feeling of
my heart
igniting and fracturing
at the same time?
This is more than just a broken heart.
This is the type of pain
that causes you to lose yourself.

Where can I find a
remedy for this?
No amount of rest can
cure this torment.
Bitterness seems inexorable.
Impending virulence
fragmentizes my hope.

Bad Again

My upper thigh
starts to buzz
whenever I get bad again.

My body feels like
it's trying to tempt me
whenever I get bad again.

At times I feel
my thigh begin to itch
whenever I get bad again.

I try to forget
how I used to cope
whenever I get bad again.

I always fight against it
and try ignoring the urge
whenever I get bad again.

But the buzzing is so strong
and the temptation is fierce
and the itching is unbearable
and my prayers turn to tears
and the memories never leave
and I can't keep ignoring it-

I'm so tired of getting bad again.
I can't keep getting bad again.
It hurts getting bad again.

I pray this wasn't true.
I pray things change.

I hate getting bad again.

Change in Medication

I had to change medication again.
This time I feel stiff and suffocated.
It's like I can't move my hands or my legs.
It's like moving on is just too hard and I'm encased in thick glue.

Deserted

I'm stuck
in this desert
dying
of thirst
peace seems to
flow so freely
like a pure stream
of crystal clear water
for some
and I'm cemented
into my own reality
I crawl through the
hot
desert
sand
praying to find even
a droplet of water
but no matter
how far
it seems
I've traveled
it's always out
of my reach
peace seems
to be a mirage
to me now
so I hallucinate
happiness
and I collapse
from dehydration
letting the dark cloak
known as
hopelessness
suffocate
me
I live my days
in a paralyzed sleep
nightmarish
creatures taunt
me
who will save
me now

Trauma Email

So like, if someone could
shoot me an email
of a time period when
I'll stop feeling his hands on me-
when I'll stop hearing his grunts-
when I'll stop having flashbacks-
when the fear will go away-
when the trauma is all gone,
that'd be great!

From Human to Fish: My depression transformation

My depression turns me
into a fish with a brain disease.
I may look fine on the outside,
but from my view,
everything is moving in
slow motion and I see
everything as though I am
looking out from the
inside of a fishbowl.
The only people who know
that something is wrong with me
are the medical professionals
assigned to diagnose me
with something that sounds
too scary to say aloud.
Maybe the rest of the world
will notice something is wrong
with me when I sink to the bottom
of the tank that imprisons me,
but by then, it'll be too late.
Why is it always too late?

This is me writing to myself

This is me writing to myself and
telling myself, "You're gonna be okay,"
telling myself, "It's not your fault."
I'm trying so hard to survive.
Why can't I stop shaking?
I feel buried and
I'm trying
to dig myself out.
I'm suffocating and
gasping for air
that won't come.
Can I die from this?
I don't want to.
It's still hard to believe that
I'm that one in three.
I'm scared of all of them now.
Are they all like him?
I'm scared of all the wolves
who act so nice
until there is no one around.
Then, they steal something
so precious,
so innocent.
When it's done,
they leave you
bloodied and ashamed.
So here I am,
writing to myself,
praying that
I'm going to be okay.
I am,
I am,
I am.

"Why" Hurts

My head
Hurts
Everything
Just
Hurts
Why am I angry
why why why
why why why
why why why
again and again
why

F**k Forgiveness

Just forgive him.
You want to heal, right?
Just let it go.
You'll feel so much better
when you forgive.

But what happens when I do forgive him
and I'm not released from the pain,
the nightmares,
the flashbacks so fierce,
you forget the year?
What happens then?
What happens then?

Trauma Killers

This shell is trying to find
a will to live
at the bottom of every
prescription they give me.
Maybe the Adderall will
help me focus on the good?
Maybe the Xanax
will numb all the bad?
Maybe if I take enough Tylenol
it'll kill the trauma
along with the pain…

Part 4- An Attempted Ending

I was doing so well...

Regression was always close by
a snickering echo in my ear
forever taunting me
beckoning me near
to utter insanity
I set my soul ablaze
hoping to ignite a better path
My existence is screaming in
hope of drowning out the sound
of fate drawing near
Pains shoot across my body
(warning signs from Heaven)
telling me to change
unless I wish to go back
to that dark chasm
that sucks the spirit out of you
until you're nothing but soot
I truly was doing so well
but regression is closer
than I had imagined
I thought I'd have more time
with joy but happiness is just
a mere fleeting thought
I was doing so well
What's wrong with me now

Dead Inside

Violent whisper
Silent screams
Hallucinations
Living dreams
Broken consciousness
Waterless streams
I'm dead inside
Dead

Hopeless howling
Words amiss
Can't scream
Loneliness
Shhh
No crying
Just lying in bed

The covers enclose
Your thoughts
The saplings of depression
The only living thing
Around me
I'm dead inside
Dead

Type A Exhaustion

I don't want
to do this
anymore
I'm exhausted
of living
I'm so tired
I want to just
give up
why can't I just
give up

If I can't eat
If I can't sleep
If I can barely
breathe
What's the point
What's the use
of trying
I'm so tired
I just want to be
done
Why can't I be
done

the attempt

the shadows
oh God, the shadows
he still follows me everywhere-

the pain
oh God, the pain
i have never felt so much
pain-

the voice
oh God, the voice
i hear his voice all around me-

the pills
oh God, the pills
maybe if i take a bunch-

i wonder
how many pills
it would take to cure me?

i wonder
if i took too
many of the pills?

i wonder
why i feel
so nauseous?

i wonder
if i'll wake up
in the morning?

cold sweat

i'm shaking
and cold
so cold
so so
cold
and yet
my body sweats
releasing
making me wish
i could be
released

Stuck

I feel like I'm stuck
in that funny little moment
between life and death. When
you regret everything and
nothing at all. When you
are somehow able to accept
every event that had ever
occurred in your life, except for
what you had just done. When you
feel, hear, see, and taste
everything and nothing
at all. When you feel as though
you are everything and nothing
at all. It's almost like a sedation
and resuscitation of your heart
happening suddenly,
yet it feels like it has been
starting from the day you
were put on this Earth.

Regret

I didn't regret it is soon as I
did it. I regretted it in that
moment when it started to feel
real. In that moment when I
questioned if my life was over. In
the moment I felt I had no breath in me.

Uncertainty

It's a scary thing,
Not knowing
whether your
eyes will open
the next morning.
Will I live to see
another day?

Exhaustion Takes Me

My light
has been
smothered
for too long
just take me
Jesus
just take me
please
I'm tired
so tired
I'm done

Waking Up

Somehow, I woke up the next morning. I didn't open my eyes immediately. I guess part of me was afraid that I had died and if I opened my eyes, then I'd have to face eternity. Yet, when I opened my eyes that morning, I was surprised I was still alive. The pounding in my head accompanied by vertigo and nausea made sure to alert me I was living.

I stumbled across my residence hall to the bathroom, which was closed for cleaning. I had to use the bathroom so badly, and I felt so awful that I snuck inside regardless. The cleaning lady was nowhere in sight. As soon as I finished relieving myself, while I was still seated on the toilet, I passed out. I regained consciousness with my head resting on the back of the toilet, my arms limp by my sides, and no feeling in my legs. There was a ringing in my ears, a reminder of my mistake. I had never felt so sick before.

I held back tears until I was in my dorm room and could cry freely. What had I done? No, not me. This wasn't me. I looked at the crying girl in the streaky mirror above the dorm's sink. Who was she? She looked disgusting to me. She did not make decisions I would agree with. Her face and life had become hideously incomparable to the life that I had, or at least was supposed to have. I was supposed to be happy. I was supposed to love college and find myself. Yet, somehow, I had lost myself more than I could have ever possibly imagined. I had disgraced myself. How was God to forgive me?

Fruitless Counsel

When I was able to remotely control my tears, I called the campus's counseling center and scheduled an emergency appointment with a therapist I had never met before because that's who was on staff. I didn't know who else to go to. I was too ashamed to tell anyone I was close with, but I figured going to a counselor would be the logical thing to do. They'd know how to help me, right?

I threw up on the waiting room floor. It was an acidic solution of dissolved pills that punished my throat by burning it when it came out.

The counselor asked me several times if I had intended to try to kill myself. I told her each time that I just wanted him to go away. I told her it wasn't a suicide attempt; it was my attempt to be freed from him. I was trying to convince myself as much as I was trying to convince her. I refused to admit I had fallen to rock bottom to anyone, including myself.

The counselor called the psychiatrist that had prescribed me the medications I had taken. She told them that I overdosed and was unsure how many pills I had taken. The psychiatrist said that since I had woken up that morning and thrown up at least most of it, I didn't have to go to the hospital.

"Don't you see how lucky you are?"
"You are too young to be feeling this way."
"This can be your second chance, almost like a fresh start."

I was sent on my merry way after that appointment in which I feel as though I gained nothing. I went straight back to my dorm room and cried some more.

It took me about two years to tell my parents about my attempt. I was going to keep it from them forever, but courtrooms are open to the public, and who wants to find out that their daughter nearly killed herself in a courtroom?

Exhaustion

I am exhausted
all the time
and I am convinced
it was you
who sucked away
my energy
which was foolish because
you left something
much more dangerous,
my fight

Section Three- Survivor

Part 1- Shifting Mindset

Moving Past the Past

How do you expect to live
when you're stuck in the past?
How do you expect to move
when you don't think it will last?
Seasons come
and seasons go
but what progression
do you have to show?
Your trauma is like concrete
weighing down your feet.

Move,
body move.
Move,
body move
Why can't I just live?
God says I need to forgive.
So, I call death upon the pain.
I will live again.

Quotes from my Article- The First Half

"My entire life, I have been obsessed with being in control. Then in one night, all my control was ripped from me."

"I remember asking God why He'd allow this to happen. I remember feeling ashamed of losing control."
"The lack of fault doesn't help the victim escape any of the consequences..."
"When I felt like I was going to die, I prayed for forgiveness and for my life to turn around. Miraculously, I woke up the next morning."
"It became apparent that I had to change my environment to heal..."

"To heal, I had to address what was done to me."
"I learned how to say, 'It wasn't my fault,' and, 'The girl I have become is not one to hate. She is one to love because she is the one who carried the weight of something so horrific by herself. She survived.'"
"Although I felt weak, my persistence to keep on moving forward was the epitome of strength."
"I went from being a victim to a survivor."

Still Human

I remember everything you did to me
        I remember all the pain you've caused
I still feel the hurt
        I still feel the pain
                                                and yet
I hope you know I forgive you
        I hope you go to Heaven
I wish you no pain
        I release you from unforgiveness
        because
you're still human too

Hushed Trauma

Why should it be a secret?
Why should I feel shame?
Why should I hide it
when it wasn't my fault,
and yet you say I'm to blame?

I should've known better-
I shouldn't have…
I should just forgive him
and release myself from the pain.

How it Feels to Heal

and then it began to hail.
White orbs from heaven are
beating me into who
God wants me to be. They're
sculpting me.

Why do bad things happen…?

Not everything happens for a reason,
but we can give meaning
to even the worst
traumas that we have faced.
God's given us that power.
We just need to tap into it
and put it in use.

Why Can't I Escape You

Why won't you go away
Your body haunts mine
The darkness inside of you
Cloaked over the light inside of me
I try to wash you off me
As if that will do any good
How does one wash their soul
Their mind
Their memories
shooting through their body

Angels turn away from me
My guardian angel has left
They're scared of your darkness
A darkness that has stationed itself to my heart
A darkness so cold that it freezes my soul
A darkness so cold that it makes the demons shriek

God knows I'm a warrior
And I know that He gives His
Strongest warriors
The toughest battles
But I feel so weak
I want to give up

He reminds me that strength isn't a feeling
Strength is when I refuse to let the darkness rule over me
Strength is when I clean my soul of the trespassing shadows
Strength is when I stand by truth
Strength is an action

I will not let you consume me
I will not let you get away with your lies
I will not let you stop me from my chasing my dreams
I will not let you destroy me

I'm here to fight this battle
I refuse to lose to the darkness
I refuse to lose to the memories
I refuse to lose to you

Part 2- Resurrecting Myself

Her Reclaiming

She held a pen
and she plagiarized
perfection.
She was born
with a fire in her soul
and determination in the pit of her stomach.
She knew she could fly,
so she leaped off the cliff
and she soared with the eagles.
She is beyond existing,
she is living.
She is more than enough
because she is who she wants to be.

Melting the Ice on My Arms

There's a cold feeling
that sets in
after a panic attack.
It's like trauma freezing
to my skin and I feel
it in my arms.
I know the
forces working against
me wish my
arms would freeze into stillness.

Sadly
for them, the fire
in me scorches
my roots. Inferno
spreads over me.
I smile because
I know.
I know the ice age
will soon end.

I know I'm coming back
to myself. Thriving
was always in
my plan. So,
my enemies
have no place near
me and they
too shall leave.
They'll take with
them the ice,
but none of
the memories.

I smile gratefully
for the memories
of trauma they

leave because
I turn them into resilience.
I can finally laugh
because I know
that the ice
won't last.
It can't last. God
won't allow it.

Strength is the inferno igniting my path.
It clears my view of the future.
The ice will all soon melt away.
That isn't just my hope, it's His promise.
Ice storms are the hardest to defeat
(yet defeat is never impossible).
God's the epitome of possibilities.

So I smile through the
freezer burnt lips they
think will silence me.
I will not exist in silence.
I will live in the freedom
of my voice.
That's my choice for
living today.
That's my reason to
live today.
Despite the pain,
I'll stick it out.
Strength doesn't come
without trials and pain,
but it will come.
That's what matters.
That is not just my hope,
it's my knowledge.
No, it's more than that.
It is wisdom.

I Can Be Happy Again

Remind me to document
my happiness
in words
because it's an important
reminder
I can get there again.

God's in my Healing Body

I feel stagnant and broken
motionless
like an ocean on Mars
Far from humanity
Propose unknown
Vantage point
not seen
A slanted building
collapsing
A door left ajar
that can't quite close
Where's my hope
when I'm lost

That's when He says,
"Child," laughing
"I'm here!"
"See Me!" He muses
"Feel Me." He says more seriously
"I'll never leave you,
never."

He Sees

God sees
I seize
Drowning in the seas
Please God
Please
He smiles and just says
"These are simply the seeds."
He knows because
He sees
I can't yet see
but I will soon

I'm freed
not from the seas
I am freed from the seize
and for now
that's enough
He is enough
It is enough
Tough is
at times
enough

He smiles at my scarred body
and whispers
"You are enough."
He mends into the clouds
kissed by the sunrise
Hues of red
orange
and yellow
He sees yet
and He sees still
There is no until
He is still
Yet He moves
Yet He has power
He is power
He still smiles

Freed from my seize
My captor screeches in anger
He has lost a valuable prisoner
I'm a prisoner no more
He sees
He believes because
He knows
and soon
He will show…

I've Ceased Invoking Ignorance in Intercourse

I used to
close my eyes
every time I

let them in.
I transformed into
a mindless dream.

As though I
could erase what
was happening to

me at the
moment, and I
wished for nothingness.

For some reason,
with you I've
never felt the

urge to close
my eyes, and
I can feel.

I'm thankful
that I took
the risk to

let you close,
to my heart,
because now,

I have hope
that such fear
can end.

I am healing.
After all this
time, I'm free.

Saving Myself First

I've been praying for years
that God would show me
how to save other people.

He told me tonight that
I must first save myself.
How can I save others
when I myself am drowning?

He reminds me that being His servant
doesn't mean I'm always serving others
in finding and fulfilling their life's purpose.
I also must find and fulfill my own purpose.

Jesus showed us that preparation is
just as important as serving others.
I must be ready in order to deliver.

Growth and taking care of myself isn't a sin,
it's a commandment.
I can't wear myself down as soon as
I'm saved
or else I'll lose myself in the process.

Content vs. Satisfied

Satisfaction and being content are two different things.
Never being satisfied creates a hunger for accomplishment.
It creates a drive to meet goals and achieve dreams.
Never being content destroys your entire being.

Always work for your dreams and aspirations.
Be content with your progress at the moment.
Once the moment has passed, look towards the future.
Always keep moving forward without ceasing.

I'm satisfied with my progress, but not content,
and you know what? That's okay.

What Doesn't Kill You…

What didn't kill me
did not make me stronger-
it was attempted murder.
    However, I chose to grow
    and become stronger
    in order to move on.

Section Four- Thriver

Part 1- Chasing Justice

Interview Haiku

The first step in my
search for justice involved a
ton of interviews.

Campus Detective

I've always been afraid of the police.
This fear started when I was told,
at a very young age,
that my cousin was murdered
by a police officer.
Apparently being black and
breathing is a crime to some.

I had to tell this stranger,
a man I was subsequently afraid of,
an extremely detailed description
of what happened to me
on August 18th, 2018.

My advocate sat
to the right of me while the
detective sat directly in front of me.
He was kind enough to let me
take my time in retelling the
events of that night, but the trauma
still caused my body to shake.

I remember the cold A/C in
the desolate white interview room.
I remember him grabbing me water
while trying to help me feel more
comfortable (even though comfort
had disappeared the night of the incident.)
I remember how sweaty my palms
were from my discomfort.
I remember fighting my body and
telling it to stop feeling him on me
(I was unsuccessful.)

Before that day, I thought the most
difficult interview I'd have to endure
would be for a career.
I was sadly mistaken.

…and then I waited…

Fear in His Identification

He could be anywhere-
He could be everywhere-
He could be near-
He could be here-

When trauma is involved, Distance is a liar-

The detective said they found him-
The detective said he *shouldn't* contact me-
The detective said his part was almost done-
The detective said the worst part is nearly over-

The illusive "worst" is a liar-

The rapist said he did nothing wrong-
The rapist said it was consensual-
The rapist remained in my nightmares-
The rapist remained in my flashbacks-

The rapist is a liar-

The therapist said I *should* be safe-
The therapist said I should move on-
The therapist said I just need to meditate-
The therapist said it'll get better soon-

"Better" can only come with closure, so the therapist was a liar-

I was angry-
I was frustrated-
I was petrified-
I was distant-

I felt hope was lost, so I was a liar-

…and then I waited…

The Perfect Interviewee

I was interviewed a second time
by the campus detective.

I was interviewed a third time
by another officer at the
police station in my hometown.

I had so much experience with interviews
before I even finished college
that I considered adding it
to my extensive resumé.

Pressing Charges

I knew I needed
to press charges to prevent
another assault.

Justice needed to
be served if I ever was
to begin to heal.

One More

One more minute
Just one more breath
One more heartbeat
Before I see you again

One more smile
Just one more hello
One more step
Before I see you again

One more tear
Just one more drive
One more song
Before I see you again

Because I know
I know
I know
You'll change me again

Because I know
I know
I know
I won't be the same

Because I know
I know
I know
You'll drive me insane

Oh God how I wish
He'd disappear
With my memories
Such gruesome things

Memories I don't wish to hear
Memories I don't wish to see
Memories I don't wish to feel

I just can't see you again
I just can't
Oh God, make it stop
Oh God, make it stop

…and then I waited…

Deposition

This whole waiting thing
has me
feeling
like a
small child
waiting for
Christmas
Not a good
Christmas
either
It's like a reverse
Christmas
where there is no
joy
and the only
present
I'm getting
is an appearance on
the worst non-broadcasted
Talk Show
where I'm the
guest star
and the
host
is an attorney
I must look
presentable
for the
camera
I hate this
feeling
It won't go away
no matter how
hard I
try

The Courthouse Waiting Room

There are cracks-
On the edges of the walls-
They so fittingly painted gray-
The top of the wall-
Shines under the fluorescent lights-
And somehow-
It still seems dark-
There's a place on the wall-
Below the poster for the state helpline-
Where paint has dripped-
And it dried-
An imperfection frozen in time-
There are scuff marks on the wall-
Below the receptionist's window-
I wonder what their stories are-
And yet-
I don't want to know-

The Anger of Depositions

He didn't look at me the entire time
until I was told to look at him and identify him.
I had planned not to look at him at all.
I knew looking at the man that raped me
would only send me into a downward spiral
and that's exactly what his attorney had hoped.
I knew his attorney hoped that I'd lose strength,

but I didn't.

He sat almost directly across from me
as I fought back tears.
The look of boredom was dominant on
his face as he played on his iPad.

This happened over two years ago,
and yet, in that moment, the pain
felt so exceedingly fresh.

His attorney asked me questions
that I felt were posed to frustrate me,
and they did.
His attorney asked questions that
I felt were so specifically irrelevant
that I wanted to just be done.

But I couldn't give up.

His attorney asked what social media
platforms I had and my handles for each.
It wasn't until later that I realized he could
find me easier than ever before now that he
knew what they were.
This terrified me.
I didn't just feel in danger physically,
now I felt in danger virtually as well.

Exhaustion and distress ensued
from all the questioning
while the loud clacking of the

court reporter's typing filled the room.
I yearned for this to just be over.
I wanted all of this to just be over.

I was angry with myself for all the
questions I couldn't remember answers to.
I said "I do not recall" more times than
I could count, but how was I to remember
all the small details of two days that
took place over two years ago?

So, I remained as calm as possible.

His attorney asked if I had a good memory.
I replied, "No, but I do remember the
things that matter."
His attorney smiled as though
they had just won the case.

Little did they know that the
fight was not nearly over.

This was a duty that I signed
up for in my pursuit of justice,
yet I didn't know if I was strong
enough to go through with a trial
when this deposition was so difficult.
This was my first and only time seeing
him after the assault and I didn't know
how horribly it would make me feel
until I had to go and do it.

That's the thing though,
I did it.

…and then, while I waited…

Near Surrender

They didn't believe in me,
and I trusted them,
so I nearly didn't believe in myself.
I nearly accepted defeat
in battles my enemies
didn't have to try and fight.

They say I'm so strong,
but in the same breath,
they tell me my limits.
I nearly believed them.
Isn't that so dumb?
That I nearly believed them?
I nearly gave up on fighting.
I nearly gave up on myself.
What kind of warrior
would that have made me?

Gray Feather

I saw a gray feather
on the side of my car-
Nothing but the grace of God
holding it there-
To find a feather
is a sign your guardian angel
is with you
and God is giving you peace.

The Legal Waiting Game…

When will my advocate message me
and say,
"It's time."
I both fear and dread that moment,
yet I'm still waiting impatiently for it.
They told me the next step is
the hardest.
A trial with only God on your side,
a questioning lawyer,
an intimidating judge, and
a wondering jury.

I just want an outcome
that's just.

…but then…

About a Week Before Christmas

My new attorney called roughly a week before Christmas of 2021.
After three years and four months, the trial would finally occur.
The trial was set for a few days after Christmas.
The pain and tears that I thought were all gone came back so suddenly.
The kindness and sincerity in her voice gave me hope that things would be okay.

...so then, before...

The Trial

I decided that I would only have
my great aunt in the courtroom
with me as I testified.
I didn't want my parents to
have to go through that trauma,
they've already been through enough.

…and then, finally came…

The Day I Testified

Blurred reality
in and out of my body
in and out of the present
I need to breathe
I need to breathe

I didn't want my parents in the courtroom
I couldn't put them through that
I couldn't hold back the sobbing
if I saw them in those benches
with pain and heartache written
all over their faces

My great aunt was the only loved one
I had in that room
While he had a large group of people

The wait was brutal
It felt like I was being tortured
just sitting outside that courtroom
My mom and great aunt were
waiting with me

I kept switching between
crying and becoming numb

I began crying again when the
victim coordinator came out
and told me it was time
I grabbed onto my mom
and she held me tight

I felt like I couldn't walk
The victim coordinator said
I had to go now
No more waiting

Walking to the front of the
courtroom as everyone waited
to hear me testify

I didn't feel like a person
I felt like a display
like an object

The county attorney went first
she was on my side
but that didn't make the
questioning any less painful
I had to be very detailed
and very explicit
Did you know they're
required to ask during
the trial if you've
ever been married to
your perpetrator

The judge on my right
the jury on my left
the county attorney to my right
the court reported in front of me
he was also in front of me
I didn't want to look at him
it would be too much
but I couldn't stop myself
because maybe he would
seem remorseful
but he only looked
annoyed and bored

His attorney then asked
a multitude of questions
I remained polite
but some of her
questions were frustrating me
They were so specific and
irrelevant to the trauma
Does it really matter what I ate
for breakfast that morning

There was a gasp from the jury
when I stated that I was
a virgin before he assaulted me

My great aunt later told me
that one of the male jurors
had to brush tears away
when I testified

When I cried
I made the mistake of
looking at the people he
brought to support him
one of the girls rolled her eyes
at me as I tried to gain control
over my tears
I found it nearly impossible
to breathe at times

There were two breaks
that had to be taken
in order for me to watch footage
One was of me in the ER
the day after I was assaulted
and being questioned by police
The other was of my first interview
with the campus detective
My great aunt had to hold me both times
as I sobbed in her arms uncontrollably
It all felt like too much
and I just wanted to give up
I just wanted it all to be done
All while he sat on his phone
and cracked jokes with his attorney
I could barely breathe
He was so close
and my body wouldn't allow
me to calm down
because it remembered what he did
to me and it told me that I wasn't safe

When I was finally done testifying
I left the courtroom and nearly
collapsed on the elevator door
because my legs didn't

feel strong enough to hold
my body and all the pain
it was carrying
My great aunt held me
and tried to comfort me

Strangers and a rapist
I had to share such
detailed
traumatizing
personal
and agonizing events
in a room full of
strangers
and the man that raped me

But I did it

…It made me feel like a…

Porcelain Doll

Porcelain doll
Porcelain doll
Oh, how pretty you look
reflected in the brown marble wall

Are you truly that pale
Or do the court lights
shine so brightly they
mask your beauty like a veil

Porcelain doll
Porcelain doll
Oh, how pretty you look
and from the jury's view, how small

…and then I faced a…

Destroyed Sanctuary

When I was in therapy, right after it happened, my therapist had me create a safe space within my mind.

I would imagine a wooded forest with a night sky full of stars. She told me to create a mansion with many rooms to house the versions of myself that experienced trauma. She told me to create a hot tub to clean those versions of myself before they went into the mansion. She told me to create a dumpster with an unbreakable lock to put the bad memories inside. She told me to create a stage to play out the traumatic memories before I separated myself from them in my mind.

Once I separated myself from them then I would put the bad stuff in the dumpster and lock it tight. I would talk to that version of myself and ask her what her age was and how she was feeling at that moment. I would then tell her my age and that I am safe now and that she is as well. I would put her in a hot tub to wash her of the bad things that happened to her. I'd make her clean from the gritty pain. I then gave her clothes and walked her to her room where she would have everything she could possibly want and need to be happy. Then I would open my eyes and move on with my life.

But when I had to testify in a courtroom in front of him I lost the peace I had worked so hard on achieving. That wound was torn open again and it was worse than it had ever been before. Last night I couldn't stop thinking about how bored he looked while watching me cry in front of everybody when I had to relive what he did to me.

I went back to that place in my mind again and I began to tear everything apart. The dumpster was already ajar. I threw everything I could get my hands on while I screamed and cried harder and louder than I ever could bring myself to do physically. The mansion was torn apart and I don't recall seeing those versions of myself anymore. What was happening to them? They must be hiding from the monsters running rampant in my mind. They must be so terrified. I was so terrified. How was I ever supposed to find them all and make them clean and safe again?

How was I ever going to make them feel at peace again? I felt like I had failed in my duty of saving them.

The hot tub was out of water. There was nowhere for me to clean myself of the bad. The evergreens in the forest were dying and the stars didn't seem to be shining very brightly anymore. The stars fell like bombs from the sky. My utopia had become a warzone.

I wonder if I'll ever be able to find peace again. I wonder if I'll ever be able to repair the brokenness again because right now there is no peace, happiness, or cleansing waters to save me. He left me with something far more damaging and it's not sadness or depression. No, it's far worse than that. He left me with only pain and an agony that I don't know how I will overcome or if I will even be able to do so because despite them telling me that I'm so strong, I know that I have my limits. I am afraid of pushing myself farther than I already have when I had to testify in court that day.

Murder- Twice Over

He killed the girl I was that night
and I've fought so hard
the past three and a half years
to get her back.

When I testified in court last week
and I saw the boredom on his face
while I had to relive that day,
he killed me again.

There should be a law against that.
A law against killing a person's identity.
But then again,
when has justice ever been in my favor?

…and then, I wrote…

The Pain of Justice

To whoever understands,

I don't really know who you are or how this letter will get to you, but I have so many questions and I just don't know who to go to. Before I ask you the questions that are haunting me, I need to give you a little background. I don't want to go into too much detail because it's too hard reliving everything again. I just can't do that right now. I don't have it in me to relive it again today.

Last Wednesday I had to testify in front of a court full of strangers. Besides the judge, court reporter, and attorneys, half were the jury and the other half consisted of him and his friends and family. The only person that loved me in that room was my great-aunt. I told my parents not to come in because it would be far too painful. I didn't want to ask any other friends or family because it was four days after Christmas and three days until the New Year. I didn't want any more pain to come out of this if I could help it.

I cried so many times the week and a half leading up to it. That's all the advance notice they gave me. I tried to get through my testimony, but it was so hard. Part of me wishes there was someone I knew that could understand this pain, but that's far too selfish a thought. They made me use such vulgar language. I knew it was so there was no confusion that he raped me, but it made me cry. Can you believe that after 3 years, 4 months, and 11 days that it still can feel as painful as it was the day that I woke up sober and remembered bits and pieces of what he did to me the night before? I hope the jury does at least because I don't even want to think of how painful it may be if they don't-

When the state attorney asked me if I had had any other sexual interactions before and I told her no, one of the women on the jury gasped. The state attorney had me explain how I tried to get up because I knew something was wrong, but I was so weak that when he pushed my left shoulder down, I couldn't move. I couldn't fight him. I didn't want it. I didn't want any of it. I don't want this. I don't want any of this. Yet here I am, writing a letter I don't know what I'm going to do with. Anyways, after I said that, my aunt told me that she saw a young man on the jury wipe a tear away. I'm praying that's a good sign, but there's so much out of my control. I hate that. I hate all of this

To get to the point, I just want to know if it's always going to be like this. Is there always this constant cycle of pain? It's been nearly three and a half years, and yet, at times, I forget that I'm not eighteen anymore. Do you know how awful it feels to have to remind yourself how old you are, and where you are, and struggle telling yourself you're safe because you just don't know if that's true? Do you know? Do you know what it feels like to be in such agony, yet you can't cry so you just hear yourself screaming and crying in your head? Do you know? Is this what justice looks like? Is this what justice feels like? If so, I would trade justice for peace and happiness any day. I'm so close to giving up. I don't think I have enough fight in me to care anymore. I can't keep existing like this. I want to move on. I need to move on. Do you know when I can move on? Do you know when it gets better? I'm trying. I'm trying so f***ing hard. But, I don't feel like trying to do anything anymore because when I looked out that day, even though I told myself not to, I looked into his eyes. I saw boredom there. The kind of boredom you have at math class and the teacher is droning on about integrals. What the f**k am I fighting for anymore? Please, give me one good reason to keep fighting and I will. I just don't know if I can anymore. I'm so tired. There's such a large part of me that wants to just give up. They tell me I'm so strong for getting through this, but I don't want to get through this. Is this what fighting feels like? If so, I'd rather just sleep. God, I want to sleep so badly and not be terrorized by thoughts of him being found "innocent" by the jury and him finding me for payback. Will I be strong enough to fight him now? Will I be strong enough to stop him now? Please, just give me a good reason to keep going despite the pain now because I'm struggling to find one good enough. I hope you don't understand my pain, but if you do, please give me some answers because I can't do this anymore, I just can't.

Sincerely,

Whoever the f*** I am anymore

… I sat with these feelings until…

The Verdict

He was found guilty two days after my 22nd birthday.
I felt so much weight lifted off of me.
Feelings of relief, safety, and security welcomed me.
These were feelings that I hadn't felt in nearly three and a half years.
Those that were close to me could see a change in me- for the better this time.
I'd walked through the valley of darkness and come out lighter than ever before.
My light was a direct rebuttal to all the struggles I'd faced before.
Now, I wanted to live.
Now, I was no longer chained to this trauma.
Now, I didn't feel such intense pain.
Now, I was joyful.
Now, I could separate my identity from this situation.
I was no longer a victim or a survivor, I am just me.
I knew then that all of my fighting was worth it.
I was so freed.
Instead of making those tearful despairing calls to my loved ones
when I told them that I'd been assaulted,
I was calling to tell them I had been liberated
and that I could finally move on,
and I did just that.

I felt stronger than I had ever felt before.
It was almost completely done.
I had stuck through the hardest moments
and I had won the war.
I had beaten so many odds.
I was given a .5% chance of this outcome
and I had made it.
I was free.

The News

There was news coverage after the trial.
I had learned that when the verdict came
and he was found guilty,
he lifted his face shield and
kissed his girlfriend
before being escorted into
custody by the police.

I was relieved to find
that my identity was kept
hidden from society
and I had control over who
knew what happened to me
while he was being held accountable
for his actions, finally.
His picture was on nearly
every article.

The Final Step

The last thing I had to do
was read my victim impact statement
at his sentencing hearing.
Over three and a half years later,
I finally had the opportunity to
express the impact of the assault
on me and those that I loved.
I could choose whether or not
I would address him directly
when I read this statement
aloud in a courtroom full of people.
I was ready though.
The worst of it was over.
Although he still refused to look at me,
I read the final part of my statement
while looking directly at him.
It was my time to be heard
and heard I was.

My Victim Impact Statement

There are two versions of myself: the girl I was before I was raped and the person I was after. The people that knew me in high school would describe me as the shy nerdy girl that played violin and actually liked going to class every day. Before I went off to college I had worked as a dietary aide at a nursing home for nuns. My boss at the time said that I had the perfect disposition to work specifically with the nuns that had Alzheimer's and dementia and I loved doing so. I was a nearly straight-A student, a member of a few honor societies, a junior all-state violinist, and strongly connected in my journey with God. Most of all, I had this passion for life and excitement for the journey ahead of me. When I woke up the morning after I had been assaulted, that girl was gone, and I was so afraid that she'd never return.

August 18th, 2018 I was sexually assaulted in my dorm room at the University of... When I woke up the next morning and looked at the purity ring on my finger, I remembered what had occurred that night, and I had to make the hardest phone call to my mom I had ever made. The news broke their hearts. My parents then drove an hour and a half from… to take me to the hospital where I was examined and found to have injuries in areas I hesitate to mention aloud. I had to be swabbed in these places and pictures were taken of these injuries. I have never been made to feel so less than human in my entire life. I had to retell the incident to multiple officers, physicians, and my own parents. I didn't eat that entire day.

I remember telling my parents to leave and holding back tears until it was nighttime, and I could muffle my cries in darkness when I thought my roommate was asleep. I didn't sleep much that night because every time I closed my eyes, I felt him on me. Keeping my eyes open wasn't helping because I saw his shadow everywhere. These flashbacks and the fear that I experienced are something that I still deal with to this day, not to mention the awful nightmares that I had about the horrific act that he committed. Over three and half years later, I still can't escape that night. I had to go to countless therapy sessions before I learned how to ground myself when I have flashbacks and wake up in the middle of the night because of nightmares I had about the incident. I felt like I was going crazy because I would see his shadow everywhere. I was so paranoid that I was going to get hurt again and I had to keep telling myself that I was safe, that everything was going to be alright. I could never fully convince myself of this because I was never really sure if it was even true. I had no way of knowing I was safe and nothing felt alright.

I had to take weeks off of school, drop two of my courses, and I failed one course. I had never come close to failing a class before. I am a perfectionist, especially when it comes to my education, and when I failed that class it felt like I had become a completely different person. They say that after a person experiences trauma, their mind changes. They are a new person. I felt that shift in me as well and I didn't feel like I had control of whom I had become. I hated that girl who couldn't get out of bed until noon most days and stayed in bed nearly all day. I hated that girl who would do anything to numb the pain, anything to forget what happened to her. I hated the girl who couldn't get to class half of the time. I hated the girl who wanted so badly for his shadows to go away that she would overdose in her dorm room, somehow wake up the next morning, and only be brave enough to tell a counselor. I hated that girl and I prayed to God that I could find myself again. I prayed to God that whatever part of me was lost that night could come back because I couldn't live like that for much longer. I prayed to God and asked Him why such an awful thing would happen to me. I felt so disconnected from myself, I asked people to stop calling me "Katrina" and refer to me as "Kat." Katrina was gone indefinitely.

Going back to the University of... for my second semester in college, I couldn't take it anymore. I was too afraid. So, after being back on campus for a few days, I dropped out of ... and had to move back home with my parents. Not being on the same campus where he assaulted me didn't stop the flashbacks and nightmares, I continued therapy back in ... and pushed myself to take classes and move on, but it still feels like a part of me is stuck in that night and I didn't know how to move past it. Everyone who knew me saw a definite change in me. I was not the same person they sent off to college.

Over three and a half years later, no matter how hard I keep trying to make my brain forget what happened to me, my body continues to remind me of that night. My anxiety spikes when any man is behind me. There are still times at night when I feel the weight of his body on mine and his hand on my left shoulder keeping me from getting up. I'm terrified of having children because if I were to have a girl, I'd always be terrified that she'd go through what I had to endure. There are times when the flashbacks and nightmares still get so intense that I have to remind myself where I am at, how old I am, and that I should be safe. It's hard to convince myself that I am safe from a person that wasn't held accountable for such a dehumanizing and traumatic event that was only his choice, not mine. I was powerless and he took advantage of that I work as hard as I can every day to gain that power back, but I'm not naive enough to believe that I'll ever be the same again.

When I made the decision to press charges, I knew I wanted two things: Justice and for no other girl to have to go through all of the pain and loss that I had to go through because of him. Pain and loss felt not only by me but also by my friends, family, and all those people that care about me. After nearly three and a half years, what felt like a lifetime, the time finally came for me to testify in court. The nightmares and flashbacks got worse as soon as I found out when I was supposed to testify, which was right before Christmas of last year. When I testified, even though I knew it was probably a bad idea, I looked at him. I told myself that maybe if I saw some signs of remorse or any inkling of emotion on his face, I'd feel more at peace with knowing that his guilt would prevent him from hurting another girl. However, when I looked at him as I was trying to speak through my tears while reliving that night and retelling it to a room full of strangers again, I saw nothing besides what I can only describe as boredom. Not to mention that during the breaks we took the day I testified when I was forced to rewatch videos of me the morning after the assault in the hospital being questioned by campus police and in my first interview with Detective Jaeger, I vividly remember the defendant laughing, at what, I do not know, while my great aunt held me in her arms as I cried. It finally struck me that what he did to me meant nothing to him. He could care less about the destruction his actions had on my life. At that moment, I felt like I had gone back to square one and I was that same eighteen-year-old girl in her dorm room aching and crying and begging for the pain to stop. I felt as though he had murdered that young girl again, just as I was getting her back.

In regard to his sentencing, I'm asking that the Court give the defendant a punishment that is befitting and equitable to the severity of the crime he committed and the pain and disorder that was caused upon me and those I love as a result of it.

To the defendant I say: You know what you did to me that night. What you did was wrong. You knew I couldn't fight back, yet you completely disregarded my humanity. I have to live with the consequences of a choice you made for the rest of my life. A decision that you made that was completely against my will and I was unable to fight against. I am somebody and the mental, financial, physical, academic, social, and emotional wounds that you've caused me to have, I'll have to deal with them for the rest of my life. I hope you'll reflect on everything I've shared today and never forget one word of it. Whether or not you ever begin to understand this pain that you've forced upon me, I pray that no one else falls victim to you the way that I did.

Outcome

He was given the maximum sentence in prison
and had to pay for all the medical bills
and other expenses that I acquired as a result
of the assault.

I recognize that this isn't always the outcome,
but I know that if I didn't at least try
I would have always regretted it.
It is a decision every person who has
been assaulted has to face,
and that was just mine.
No decision is right
and no decision is wrong.
That was just the decision
I had to make for myself
in order to fully heal.
While others may only
fully heal if they don't have to
face the trauma of a trial.
I'm glad that I didn't
let the doubting of my strength
hold me back from fighting.

I did it.
I am strong.
I am not happy that this happened to me,
yet I can still be proud of myself for having
overcome such a monstrous obstacle.

Two Rabbits and a Note from God

Two days after the sentencing trial I had to watch the movie "Ma Rainey's Black Bottom" on a Wednesday evening with one of my classes. As Levee, one of the characters, began to describe the rape of his mother, I felt myself tense up. He talked about the men taking his mother's body because of their entitlement, desire, and greed. I left the room and barely made it to the bathroom before I broke out in tears. I cried in a stall for ten minutes. I looked at myself in the mirror in anger while trying to dry my tears. I was supposed to be over this, he was in jail now. What else did I need? The movie ended with Ma in the back of the car discontent because she knew that the men she worked for had used her and could care less about her humanity. I saw his face then. I saw him laughing as he walked past me crying while my mother held me as he was escorted out of the courtroom to prison. I felt defeated.

I drove back home to find two rabbits sitting in my front yard, staring at me. I sat in my car wondering why they'd be out in the rain and weren't scared away by my car. We sat and looked at each other for a long while. I looked up the meaning behind seeing two rabbits since it felt significant, and I don't believe in coincidences. I read that seeing two rabbits meant that regardless of what you're going through, you are strong, even though you may not feel like it. We can find strength in ourselves, even if we can't see it immediately. I walked into my room to find a quote I stuck to my wall fallen in front of my door. The quote told me that I needed to move on from my past and love myself the way I deserved to be loved. I told God I heard Him.

As I showered, I washed myself clean of my past. I had been telling myself not to let things bother me for more than 5 minutes if they wouldn't be painful in 5 years. I told myself I was stronger than letting what he did to me be painful any longer. I began to pray and tell the Devil he was done pulling me back. I am stronger than that. The love of God that is found within me is stronger than he will ever be. Therefore, I am stronger than he will ever be because I have God on my side. I am free from his torments and the pain he tried to place on my life. I will no longer be a prisoner to shame, guilt, flashbacks, nightmares, and pain. I am stronger than that. I will move forward with my chin up and a look of determination on my face. I will not let others' actions and wrongdoings control me. I am worth more than that. I am a warrior. That battle has been fought and I will move on because I deserve that. I deserve to be happy and love myself enough to chase what I desire with God by my side and with God in my heart. I am moving on. I have found my peace and freedom. In Jesus' name.

Part 2- Society's Response

The Creation and Alleviation of Perpetrators

Perpetrators are created
systematically-
So why does society try to fix them
discretely?

These men aren't the
elusive shadows
we read about in books-
they are
our neighbors-
what are they teaching our children about "home"?
our teachers-
what are they teaching our children when we leave the classroom?
our so-called leaders-
what are they teaching our children what greatness is?
our so-called defenders-
what are they teaching our children what power is?
our co-workers-
what are they teaching our children what boundaries are?
our friends-
what are they teaching our children what healthy relationships are?
our family-
what are they teaching our children what love is?

To alleviate the epidemic of perpetrators,
are we to
detach
or
ATTACK
this "normalcy"?

They want to know

They want to know
The truth
until
they don’t

Considering

"You're doing so well!"
They tell me,
until they see my mask falter.
They fear my response,
a subtle hint of a frown
"Well, considering..."

Honesty's Repercussions

I fear the consequences of truth
I fear your disbelief
and the denial that may come
unless you already know
what happened to me
happened to you
Oh God, don't let it be so
Forgive me for not telling you sooner
and making you process it in an awful place
I'm sorry I can't even tell you
Oh God, I'm such a disgrace
I pray I was braver
I pray I was stronger
I pray I was wiser too
because I know my lack of
possessing these things
have only hurt you
I'm so sorry
Brother,
I'll forever love you

I Fear Telling You What Happened to Me

Don't push me away
when I tell you
all that was done to me
all the pain I've endured
could've caused a rose to bleed

Don't make me say
I'm sorry
for all the discomfort
my honesty has caused
because my past isn't pretty
and neither are my scars
Don't make me regret opening up
for the first time in my life
I'm trying to escape
the shame
and all the hurt that lies inside
My heart is too big to hate you
for drawing away from me
because you fear the life I've lived
so much for honesty

"It's such a pity..."

I can read your mind.
Your eyes say it all,
and I hate that.

Pity Sickens Me

Don't look at me with pity.

Pity is for the weak.
Unless you're trying
to insult me by
calling me weak then
don't look at me with pity.

Pity is for the weak.
If you really knew me,
then you'd know
that I'm anything but.

Pitiful Gazes

"I hate it."
        "Hate what?"
"That look of pity
in their eyes when I tell
them what happened.
I feel like I can read
their minds at that
very moment.
'Poor girl' They think.
'Such a shame.'
'How awful a thing to happen
at such a young age.'"
        "And what do you think?"
"I think we're all screwed
in some way or another."

Don’t pity me.

Understand me,
Know me.
See me-
Not what was done to me.
Listen to me-
Not just a police report.
Look at me-
Not just at my scars.
Be present with me-
Don’t let your mind wander
To wonder about the details.
Know me-
All of me…

Regrets

My top five regrets:

1. When I chose to paint my room "Rocker Girl Pink" in elementary school. I quickly grew to despise the bright color.
2. That time I got a matching tattoo with a girl I considered a sister. We are no longer friends anymore and the tattoo is permanent across half of my thigh.
3. A few years ago, I allowed one of my friends to give me bangs and a haircut. She only cut three-quarters of my bangs and my hair was so uneven that three inches were trimmed off to fix it.
4. The fact that I ever thought that dating a wannabe rapper was a good idea. He would only ever talk about his rap career and played me the most hideous raps he created. Needless to say, his career died quickly, along with our relationship.
5. When I shaved half of my hairline off as a kid because I thought the razer was cool. I tried hiding it from my parents in fear of being punished. Of course, my mom noticed and she was not pleased, to say the least.

Notice how that list doesn't include being raped? That's because using the word "regret" implies I feel poorly about a decision that I made. Since I didn't choose to be raped, I cannot classify that as a regret. I'm glad we can agree, esteemed defense attorney, that rape and regret are two different things. (Thank you so much for saying that by the way because the press graciously made sure to report your direct quote to emphasize our consensus.) However, "regret" doesn't begin to classify what occurred that night. No need to take my word for it though, I'm sure the judge can define "guilty" for you if you'd like.

They tell me I'm the perfect ~Survivor~

A smile on my face,
I go to class.
Nothing is wrong with me!

I go to therapy, but I don't
Need to, right?
I stay busy with extracurriculars.
What a good girl!

Heck, I can even crack a joke
Once in a while!
Maybe I'll even start a new
Social justice movement!

What a champ!
I'm doing so well!
Round of applause for me!
Bravo!

Does it even matter

When you asked me
what ethnicity he was,
I felt defeated.

Does it even matter
    if he was black or white?
    how old he was?
    where he was from?
    how he was raised?
    what religion he was?
    what I was wearing?
    if I said yes to a dance?
    if I knew him?

Does it even matter?

Certainty

"Are you sure?"
        I freeze at the words.
        Am I sure
                what he did to me was wrong?
                that I didn't want any part of it?
                that these memories will haunt me forever?
                that now I'm afraid to be alone?
                that I see the world differently?
                that I see men differently?
                that I suffocate at the thought of him?
"Yes, I am sure."

Would You?

Would you still
love me
if I told you
What happened to me?
Would you stay
or
say I'm too broken?

Part 3- For the Fighters

Courageous Living

It takes courage
to live in a world
that has hurt you so-
But you must live.
You must…

Control What You Can

You're not stubborn, you're just tired of losing control. Remember to trust your journey and that if you don't have control over one thing, then it's okay to allow yourself the freedom and peace to do what brings you joy. That is something you can have control of, even in your most chaotic moments.

Claim Your Hope in Change

Claim
your peace
your joy
your freedom
Become bold
This shall start
your revival
and God will
manifest Himself
like never before
and you will
manifest yourself
like never before

There's hope
There is hope
There has to be hope

Change course
from the path of death
to the path of light
the path of light
the path of life

Revival is on its way
to you
Out of bondage
into freedom
Out of slavery
into the light

Seek truth
about who you are
His heart is turned
towards you
He hears you

Receive His word
and create a battle plan
because you're a warrior

and He’s preparing you
for battle
because you’re strong
You are
even if you don’t feel like it
you are
There’s hope for you
There is

Quotes from my Article- The Second Half

"I have gone from a survivor to a thriver. There is a refreshing sort of freedom that comes from that."
"I have learned how to love others again."
"I have learned how to love myself again."
"I recognize that I can't erase what happened to me by numbing myself using sex or alcohol. I just need to find healthy ways to cope and grow."
"Healing is not linear."
"Healing takes time. I just need to have patience and the strength to endure the present."
"So, what would I say to those out there who have gone through what I have? It's not your fault, even if it might feel like it is. You didn't ask for this, no matter what others may say. No one can take your fight away from you, and your fight can always be summoned. It's okay to backtrack as long as you set your eyes on moving forward. It's okay to reach out for help because there's always someone out there wanting to help you. You can overcome this, and you will. You just need to believe and put in the work."

"It's not fair or right, but it does get better. You are stronger than you can imagine. Your hope is the cornerstone of your healing. Find what you can control because that will be integral to finding your happiness again. I love and believe you. Please, don't ever give up."

Attainable

I am grateful for all those that supported me-
My friends, family, professors, and co-workers
that met me with love when I needed it the most.

I am grateful for therapy
which gave me the tools
I needed to cope.

I am grateful for the doctors
that gave me medications
to take the edge off
when I wasn't able to do so myself.

I stopped fearing the word "help"
because I recognized that I would
not receive it if I stayed silent.

I recognized my strength
and the attainability of
peace, wholeness,
oneness, and complete healing,
and so I became all of these things.

I urge the fighters to lean on these things,
when standing seems too difficult.
I urge fighters to look to these things,
when getting out of bed feels impossible.
I urge the fighters:
    Recognize your strength
    You can find peace-
    You can be whole again-
    You can be one with yourself again-
    You can be completely healed-
as long as you recognize and pursue these things,
then they will come to you,
slowly but surely,
they will come.

Crown Thyself

Your crown is in your hands.
Nobody's words or actions
can make you any less than
what you want to be.

Throw the crown down and
accept a lesser life and
a lesser attainment of self-

Hold the crown and
wait for others to give you
your highest self and your life-

Crown thyself
and make thyself and thy light
radiantly powerful.

Letting Go Vs. Releasing

Looking at Her through eyes pooling with tears, I realized something-
"It's not about letting it go.
You've given so much power and energy to past situations and circumstances by trying to force yourself to let them go.
Their hold on you got stronger because of it."

I saw Her heart break at my words-
I felt Her heart break as though it was my own-

"You must release these things.
You must release control, for you cannot control the past.
You must release fear, for you should not fear what has already passed.
You must release guilt, for you cannot face a future when you're in bondage to the past.
You must release alternate scenarios for you cannot change what has already passed.
Do you hear me?"

She nodded Her head and sighed.
I wiped away Her tears, moved away from the mirror, and turned off the light.
I refused to see Her again after that night.

Final Message

You can and you will heal
You just need to fight
I know you didn't choose to be a warrior
I know it's hard
but I believe in you
Please believe in yourself
and just fight

Made in the USA
Coppell, TX
14 March 2023